# A W  the ROSARY

How to Pray the Rosary

*including*

The Mysteries of Light

Sister Mary Francis P.C.C.

McCRIMMONS
Great Wakering, Essex

This edition first published in United Kingdom in 2003 by
McCRIMMON PUBLISHING COMPANY LIMITED
10-12 High Street, Great Wakering, Essex SS3 0EQ, England.
Telephone 01702-218956  Fax 01702-216082

Email: mccrimmons@dial.pipex.com
Website: www.mccrimmons.com

Original edition of *How to Pray the Rosary* was first published
in United Kingdom in 1975 by
Mayhew-McCrimmon Ltd.

© 1975, 1999, 2003 McCrimmon Publishing Company Ltd.

ISBN 0 85597 648 9

---

Nihil Obstat

Martin Hancock
David Donnelly

Imprimatur
Brentwood January 30 1975

C.D. Creede Vic. Gen.

---

*Acknowledgements*

The scripture texts are taken from the *Jerusalem Bible* published and copyright 1966, 1967 and 1968 by Darton, Longman and Todd Ltd, and used by permission of the publishers.

Typeset in Clearface regular 11/12.5pt and Aesop 22pt
Cover design Alan Hencher and Nick Snode
Printed in the United Kingdom by Optech Printing Ltd., Basildon, Essex

# Contents

Introduction . . . . . . . . . . . . . . . . . . . . . . . . . . . . . . . 5
The Prayers of the Rosary . . . . . . . . . . . . . . . . . . . . . 9

## THE JOYFUL MYSTERIES
    The Annunciation . . . . . . . . . . . . . . . . . . . . . . . . 10
    The Visitation . . . . . . . . . . . . . . . . . . . . . . . . . . 12
    The Nativity . . . . . . . . . . . . . . . . . . . . . . . . . . . 15
    The Presentation . . . . . . . . . . . . . . . . . . . . . . . . 18
    The Finding in the Temple . . . . . . . . . . . . . . . . . . 21

## THE MYSTERIES OF LIGHT
    Christ's Baptism
        in the Jordan River . . . . . . . . . . . . . . . . . . . . 23
    Christ's Self-Manifestation
        at the Marriage of Cana . . . . . . . . . . . . . . . . . . 25
    Christ's Proclamation of the Kingdom of God
        with His Call to Conversion . . . . . . . . . . . . . . . . 27
    Christ's Transfiguration
        when He revealed His Glory to His Apostles . . . . . . 30
    Christ's Institution of the Eucharist as the
        Sacramental Expression of the Paschal Mystery . . . . 32

## THE SORROWFUL MYSTERIES
- The Agony in the Garden .................... 35
- The Scourging of Jesus at the Pillar ........... 38
- The Crowning of Jesus with Thorns .......... 40
- Jesus Carries His Cross ..................... 43
- The Crucifixion .......................... 45

## THE GLORIOUS MYSTERIES
- The Resurrection ......................... 48
- The Ascension ........................... 51
- The Descent of the Holy Spirit ............... 54
- The Assumption of Our Lady ................ 57
- The Crowning of Our Lady in Heaven ......... 60

Prayer ................................. 63

# Introduction

This third edition of *A Way to Pray the Rosary,* formerly entitled *How to Pray the Rosary,* now includes the new Mysteries of Light.

No longer do we leave the Joyful Mysteries when Jesus was twelve years old to next join him at the end of his life in Gethsemane in the Sorrowful Mysteries. The Mysteries of Light bridge that time gap in the life of our Saviour. We join him first at his Baptism in the river Jordan then through his public life concluding with the Last Supper, and so now we can follow him from the Upper Room to Gethsemane for the Sorrowful Mysteries. The Glorious Mysteries usher in the triumph of the Cross in our Saviour's Resurrection.

Each decade or mystery has a special message, but every one reveals to us more deeply God's love for us, his sending of his only-begotten Son down to earth for love of us, his life, Passion and death for love of us, and then in the Glorious Mysteries, we ponder on the consummation of it all; the end which is the beginning, and in which, in the Mystical Body we are each incorporated.

As we pray the rosary, the role of Our Lady in our salvation will also come to have an ever deepening meaning for us; from her first humble acceptance in the Annunciation, to become the Mother of God, to her acceptance on Calvary to be the Mother of all the children of God, the brethren of her Divine Son. With Jesus, Mary too is with us always.

In the third Eucharistic Prayer of the Mass, we pray, "Strengthen in faith and love your Pilgrim Church…" Was it not for this purpose that Our Lady introduced to St. Dominic the devotion or prayer which we call the Rosary? Is it any less relevant to our needs today, when the faith and love of the Pilgrim Church are so much in need of strengthening? It is to our great loss then if we reject it.

*A Way to Pray the Rosary* was originally written in response to the needs of so many who were struggling with distractions when praying the Rosary, some were abandoning it altogether as hopeless for them. Those who are familiar with the previous two editions will need no introduction to this format for praying the Rosary.

Again, the quotations given for all the Mysteries are only offered as one suitable selection for each Mystery. There are so many other passages to choose from that some may prefer to select others they personally find more helpful. Such rosaries can open a gateway into the Scriptures, where the Word of God is experienced anew not only as 'living and active' but awaiting us.

Finally, in the Holy Father's Apostolic Letter 'Rosarium Virginis Mariae' he writes:

> 'According to current practice, Monday and Thursday are dedicated to the "joyful mysteries", Tuesday and Friday to the "sorrowful mysteries", and Wednesday, Saturday and Sunday to the "glorious mysteries". Where might the "mysteries of light" be inserted? If we consider that the "glorious mysteries" are said on both Saturday and Sunday, and that Saturday has always had a Marian flavour, the second weekly meditation on the "joyful mysteries", mysteries in which Mary's presence is espe-

cially pronounced, could be moved to Saturday. Thursday would then be free for meditating on the "mysteries of light".'

The full text of the Holy Father's letter is now available. It will inspire and enrich our devotion beyond measure.

May Our Lady, Queen of the most holy Rosary, pray for us.

*Sr. Mary Francis.*

Sr. Mary Francis P.C.C.

Poor Clare Monastery, Bulwell, Nottingham

# The Prayers of the Rosary

The prayers used in the rosary, for those not familiar with them, are:-

\*\*\*

Our Father who are in heaven, hallowed be thy name. Thy kingdom come. Thy will be done on earth as it is in heaven. Give us this day our daily bread, and forgive us our trespasses, as we forgive those who trespass against us. And lead us not into temptation, but deliver us from evil. Amen.

\*\*\*

Hail Mary, full of grace, the Lord is with thee. Blessed art thou among women, and blessed is the fruit of thy womb, Jesus. Holy Mary, Mother of God, pray for us sinners, now, and at the hour of our death. Amen.

\*\*\*

Glory be to the Father, and to the Son, and to the Holy Spirit. As it was in the beginning, is now, and ever shall be, world without end. Amen.

# The Joyful Mysteries

## – *The Annunciation* –

Our Father.
1. In the sixth month the angel Gabriel was sent by God to a town in Galilee called Nazareth, to a virgin betrothed to a man named Joseph, of the House of David; and the virgin's name was Mary.
   *Luke 1:26-27*

   Hail Mary.

2. He went in and said to her: 'Rejoice, so highly favoured! The Lord is with you.' *Luke 1:28*

   Hail Mary.

3. She was deeply disturbed by these words and asked herself what this greeting could mean…
   *Luke 1:29*

   Hail Mary.

4. …but the angel said to her: 'Mary, do not be afraid; you have won God's favour… *Luke 1:30*

   Hail Mary.

5. 'Listen! You are to conceive and bear a son, and you must name him Jesus. He will be great and will be called Son of the Most High. The Lord God will give him the throne of his ancestor David; he will rule over the House of Jacob for ever and his reign will have no end.'   *Luke 1:31-33*

    Hail Mary.

6. Mary said to the angel, 'But how can this come about, since I am a virgin?'   *Luke 1:34*

    Hail Mary.

7. 'The Holy Spirit will come upon you,' the angel answered, 'and the power of the Most High will cover you with its shadow. And so the child will be holy and will be called Son of God.   *Luke 1:35*

    Hail Mary.

8. 'Know this too: your kinswoman Elizabeth has, in her old age, herself conceived a son, and she whom people called barren is now in her sixth month, for nothing is impossible to God.'
    *Luke 1:36-37*

    Hail Mary.

9. 'I am the handmaid of the Lord,' said Mary, 'let what you have said be done to me.'   *Luke 1:38*

    Hail Mary.

10. And the angel left her. *Luke 1:38*

    Hail Mary.

Glory be to the Father, and to the Son, and to the Holy Spirit; as it was in the beginning, is now, and ever shall be, world without end. Amen.

## – *The Visitation* –

Our Father

1. Mary set out at that time and went as quickly as she could to a town in the hill country of Judah. She went into Zechariah's house and greeted Elizabeth. *Luke 1:39-40*

    Hail Mary.

2. Now as soon as Elizabeth heard Mary's greeting the child leapt in her womb and Elizabeth was filled with the Holy Spirit. *Luke 1:41*

    Hail Mary.

3. She gave a loud cry and said: 'Of all women you are the most blessed, and blessed is the fruit of your womb. *Luke 1:42*

    Hail Mary.

4. 'Why should I be honoured with a visit from the mother of my Lord? For the moment your greeting reached my ears, the child in my womb leapt for joy. Yes, blessed is she who believed that the promise made her by the Lord would be fulfilled.' *Luke 1:43-45*

    Hail Mary.

5. And Mary said:
   'My soul proclaims the greatness of the Lord and my spirit exults in God my saviour; because he has looked upon his lowly handmaid.'
   *Luke 1:46-47*

    Hail Mary.

6. 'Yes from this day forward all generations will call me blessed, for the Almighty has done great things for me.' *Luke 1:48*

    Hail Mary.

7. 'Holy is his name, and his mercy reaches from age to age for those who fear him.' *Luke 1:49-50*

    Hail Mary.

8. 'He has shown the power of his arm,
   He has routed the proud of heart.
   He has pulled down princes from their thrones
     and exalted the lowly.

The hungry he has filled with good things,
the rich sent empty away.'  *Luke 1:51-53*

   Hail Mary.

9. 'He has come to the help of Israel his servant, mindful of his mercy – according to the promise he made to our ancestors – of his mercy to Abraham and to his descendants for ever.'

*Luke 1:54-55*

   Hail Mary.

10. Mary stayed with Elizabeth about three months and then went back home.  *Luke 1:56*

    Hail Mary.

**Glory be to the Father.**

## – *The Nativity* –

Our Father

1. Now at this time Caesar Augustus issued a decree for a census of the whole world to be taken. So Joseph set out from the town of Nazareth in Galilee and travelled up to Judea, to the town of David called Bethlehem, since he was of David's House and line, in order to be registered together with Mary, his betrothed, who was with child.
   *Luke 2:1,4-5*

    Hail Mary.

2. While they were there the time came for her to have her child, and she gave birth to a son, her first born. *Luke 2:6-7*

    Hail Mary.

3. She wrapped him in swaddling clothes, and laid him in a manger because there was no room for them at the inn. *Luke 2:7*

    Hail Mary.

4. In the countryside close by there were shepherds who lived in the fields and took it in turns to watch their flocks during the night. The angel of the Lord appeared to them and the glory of the Lord shone round them. They were terrified, but

the angel said: 'Do not be afraid. Listen, I bring you news of great joy, a joy to be shared by the whole people…'
*Luke 2:8-10*

Hail Mary.

5. 'Today in the town of David a saviour has been born to you; he is Christ the Lord. And here is a sign for you: you will find a baby wrapped in swaddling clothes and lying in a manger.'
*Luke 2:11-12*

Hail Mary.

6. And suddenly with the angel there was a great throng of the heavenly host, praising God and singing: 'Glory to God in the highest heaven, and peace to men who enjoy his favour.'
*Luke 2:13-14*

Hail Mary.

7. Now when the angels had gone from them into heaven, the shepherds said to one another: 'Let us go to Bethlehem and see this thing that has happened which the Lord has made known to us.'
*Luke 2:15*

Hail Mary.

8. So they hurried away and found Mary and Joseph, and the baby lying in the manger. When they saw the child they repeated what they had been told

about him, and everyone who heard it was astonished at what the shepherds had to say.

*Luke 2:16-18*

> Hail Mary.

9. As for Mary, she treasured all these things and pondered them in her heart. *Luke 2:19*

    Hail Mary.

10. And the shepherds went back glorifying and praising God for all they had heard and seen; it was exactly as they had been told.

    *Luke 2:20*

    Hail Mary.

**Glory be to the Father.**

## – *The Presentation* –

Our Father

1. And when the day came for them to be purified as laid down by the Law of Moses, they took him up to Jerusalem to present him to the Lord.

    *Luke 2:22*

    Hail Mary.

2. – observing what stands written in the Law of the Lord: Every first-born male must be consecrated to the Lord – *Luke 2:23*

    Hail Mary.

3. and also to offer in sacrifice, in accordance with what is said in the Law of the Lord, a pair of turtledoves or two young pigeons. *Luke 2:24*

    Hail Mary.

4. Now in Jerusalem there was a man named Simeon. He was an upright and devout man; he looked forward to Israel's comforting and the Holy Spirit rested on him. It had been revealed to him by the Holy Spirit that he would not see death until he had set eyes on the Christ of the Lord. *Luke 2:25-26*

    Hail Mary.

5. Prompted by the Spirit he came to the Temple; and when the parents brought in the child Jesus to do for him what the Law required, he took him into his arms and blessed God; *Luke 2:27-28*

    Hail Mary.

6. and he said: 'Now, Master, you can let your servant go in peace, just as you promised; because my eyes have seen the salvation which you have prepared for all the nations to see, a light to enlighten the pagans and the glory of your people Israel.' *Luke 2:28-32*

    Hail Mary.

7. As the child's father and mother stood there wondering at the things that were being said about him, Simeon blessed them *Luke 2:33-34*

    Hail Mary.

8. and said to Mary his mother: 'You see this child; he is destined for the fall and for the rising of many in Israel, destined to be a sign that is rejected – and a sword will pierce your own soul too – so that the secret thoughts of many may be laid bare.'

    *Luke 2:34-35*

    Hail Mary.

9. There was a prophetess also, Anna the daughter of Phanuel, of the tribe of Asher. She was well on

in years. Her days of girlhood over, she had been married for seven years before becoming a widow. She was now eighty-four years old and never left the Temple, serving God night and day with fasting and prayer. She came by just at that moment and began to praise God; and she spoke of the child to all who looked forward to the deliverance of Jerusalem. *Luke 2:36-38*

    Hail Mary.

10. When they had done everything the Law of the Lord required, they went back to Galilee. to their own town of Nazareth. *Luke 2:39*

    Hail Mary.

**Glory be to the Father.**

# – *The Finding in the Temple* –

Our Father

1. Meanwhile the child grew to maturity, and he was filled with wisdom; and God's favour was with him. *Luke 2:40*

    Hail Mary.

2. Every year his parents used to go to Jerusalem for the feast of the Passover. When he was twelve years old, they went up for the feast as usual.

    *Luke 2:41-42*

    Hail Mary.

3. When they were on their way home after the feast, the boy Jesus stayed behind in Jerusalem without his parents knowing it. *Luke 2:43*

    Hail Mary.

4. They assumed he was with the caravan, and it was only after a day's journey that they went to look for him among their relations and acquaintances. When they failed to find him they went back to Jerusalem looking for him everywhere. *Luke 2:44-45*

    Hail Mary.

5. Three days later, they found him in the Temple, sitting among the doctors, listening to them, and

asking them questions; and all those who heard him were astounded at his intelligence and his replies. *Luke 2:46-47*

Hail Mary.

6. They were overcome when they saw him, and his mother said to him: 'My child, why have you done this to us? See how worried your father and I have been, looking for you.' *Luke 2:48*

Hail Mary.

7. 'Why were you looking for me?' he replied. 'Did you not know that I must be busy with my Father's affairs?' *Luke 2:49*

Hail Mary.

8. But they did not understand what he meant. *Luke 2:50*

Hail Mary.

9. He then went down with them and came to Nazareth and lived under their authority. *Luke 2:51*

Hail Mary.

10. His mother stored up all these things in her heart. And Jesus increased in wisdom, in stature, and in favour with God and men. *Luke 2:52*

Hail Mary.

**Glory be to the Father.**

# The Mysteries of Light

## – Christ's Baptism in the Jordan River –

Our Father.

1. In due course John the Baptist appeared; he preached in the wilderness of Judaea and this was his message: 'Repent, for the kingdom of heaven is close at hand'. *Matthew 3:1-2*

    Hail Mary.

2. This was the man the prophet Isaiah spoke of when he said: A voice cries in the wilderness: Prepare a way for the Lord, make his paths straight. *Matthew 3:3*

    Hail Mary.

3. John said 'I baptise you in water for repentance, but the one who follows me is more powerful than I am, and I am not fit to carry his sandals; *Matthew 3:11*

    Hail Mary.

4. he will baptise you with the Holy Spirit and fire.'
   Hail Mary. *Matthew 3:11*

5. Then Jesus appeared: he came from Galilee to the Jordan to be baptised by John. *Matthew 3:13*
   Hail Mary.

6. John tried to dissuade him. 'It is I who need baptism from you' he said 'and yet you come to me!' *Matthew 3:14*
   Hail Mary.

7. But Jesus replied, 'Leave it like this for the time being; it is fitting that we should, in this way, do all that righteousness demands'. *Matthew 3:15*
   Hail Mary.

8. At this, John gave in to him. *Matthew 3:15*
   Hail Mary.

9. As soon as Jesus was baptised he came up from the water, and suddenly the heavens opened and he saw the Spirit of God descending like a dove and coming down on him. *Matthew 3:16*
   Hail Mary.

10. And a voice spoke from heaven, 'This is my Son, the Beloved; my favour rests on him'. *Matthew 3:17*
    Hail Mary.

**Glory be to the Father.**

# – Christ's Self-Manifestation at the Marriage of Cana –

Our Father.

1. Three days later there was a wedding at Cana in Galilee. The mother of Jesus was there, and Jesus and his disciples had also been invited.   *John 2:1-2*

    Hail Mary.

2. When they ran out of wine, since the wine provided for the wedding was all finished, the mother of Jesus said to him, 'They have no wine'.

    Hail Mary.   *John 2:3*

3. Jesus said 'Woman, why turn to me? My hour has not come yet.'   *John 2:4*

    Hail Mary.

4. His mother said to the servants, 'Do whatever he tells you'.   *John 2:5*

    Hail Mary.

5. There were six stone water jars standing there, meant for the ablutions that are customary among the Jews: each could hold twenty or thirty gallons. Jesus said to the servants, 'Fill the jars with water', and they filled them to the brim.

    Hail Mary.   *John 2:6-7*

6. 'Draw some out now' he told them 'and take it to the steward.' *John 2:8*

    Hail Mary.

7. They did this; the steward tasted the water, and it had turned into wine. *John 2:9*

    Hail Mary.

8. Having no idea where it came from – only the servants who had drawn the water knew – the steward called the bridegroom and said; 'People generally serve the best wine first, and keep the cheaper sort till the guests have had plenty to drink; but you have kept the best wine till now'. *John 2:9-10*

    Hail Mary.

9. This was the first of the signs given by Jesus: it was given at Cana in Galilee. *John 2:11*

    Hail Mary.

10. He let his glory be seen, and his disciples believed in him. *John 2:11*

    Hail Mary.

**Glory be to the Father.**

# – Christ's Proclamation of the Kingdom of God with His Call to Conversion –

Our Father.

1. After John had been arrested, Jesus went into Galilee. There he proclaimed the Good News from God. 'The time has come' he said 'and the kingdom of God is close at hand. Repent, and believe the Good News.' *Mark 1:14-15*

    Hail Mary.

2. The kingdom of heaven is like treasure hidden in a field which someone has found; he hides it again, goes off happy, sells everything he owns and buys the field. *Matthew 13:44*

    Hail Mary.

3. It is not those who say to me, "Lord, Lord", who will enter the kingdom of heaven, but the person who does the will of my Father in heaven.

    Hail Mary. *Matthew 7:21*

4. Then Jesus said to his disciples, 'If anyone wants to be a follower of mine, let him renounce himself and take up his cross and follow me.

    *Matthew 16:24*

'For the Son of Man is going to come in the glory of his Father with his angels, and, when he does, he will reward each one according to his behaviour'. *Matthew 16:27*

Hail Mary.

5. Then he said, 'I tell you solemnly, unless you change and become like little children you will never enter the kingdom of heaven. And so, the one who makes himself as little as this little child is the greatest in the kingdom of heaven'.

   Hail Mary. *Matthew 18:3-4*

6. Seeing the crowds, Jesus went up the hill. There he sat down and was joined by his disciples. Then he began to speak. This is what he taught them: 'How happy are the poor in spirit; theirs is the kingdom of heaven. *Matthew 5:1-3*

   Hail Mary.

7. Jesus made a tour through all the towns and villages, teaching in their synagogues, proclaiming the Good News of the kingdom and curing all kinds of diseases and sickness.

   Hail Mary. *Matthew 9:35*

8. And when he saw the crowds he felt sorry for them because they were harassed and dejected, like sheep without a shepherd. Then he said to his disciples, 'The harvest is rich but the

labourers are few, so ask the Lord of the harvest to send labourers to his harvest'. *Matthew 9:36-37*

Hail Mary.

9. So I say to you: Ask, and it will be given to you; search, and you will find; knock, and the door will be opened to you. For the one who asks always receives; the one who searches always finds; the one who knocks will always have the door opened to him. *Luke 1:9-10*

Hail Mary.

If you then, who are evil, know how to give your children what is good, how much more will the heavenly Father give the Holy Spirit to those who ask him!' *Luke 11:13*

Hail Mary.

10. But you, you must not set your hearts on things to eat and things to drink; nor must you worry. It is the pagans of this world who set their hearts on all these things. Your Father well knows you need them. No; set your hearts on his kingdom, and these other things will be given you as well. 'There is no need to be afraid, little flock, for it has pleased your Father to give you the kingdom.
*Luke 12:29-32*

Hail Mary.

**Glory be to the Father.**

## – Christ's Transfiguration when He revealed His Glory to His Apostles –

Our Father.

1. Jesus took with him Peter and James and his brother John and led them up a high mountain where they could be alone. *Matthew 17:1*

    Hail Mary.

2. There in their presence he was transfigured: his face shone like the sun and his clothes became as white as the light. *Matthew 17:2*

    Hail Mary.

3. Suddenly Moses and Elijah appeared to them; they were talking with him. *Matthew 17:3*

    Hail Mary.

4. Then Peter spoke to Jesus. 'Lord,' he said 'it is wonderful for us to be here; if you wish, I will make three tents here, one for you, one for Moses and one for Elijah.' *Matthew 17:4*

    Hail Mary.

5. He did not know what to say; they were so frightened. *Mark 9:6*

    Hail Mary.

6. He was still speaking when suddenly a bright cloud covered them with shadow, and from the cloud there came a voice which said, 'This is my Son, the Beloved; he enjoys my favour. Listen to him.' *Matthew 17:5*

    Hail Mary.

7. When they heard this the disciples fell on their faces overcome with fear. *Matthew 17:6*

    Hail Mary.

8. But Jesus came up and touched them. 'Stand up,' he said 'do not be afraid.' *Matthew 17:7*

    Hail Mary.

9. And when they raised their eyes they saw no one but only Jesus. *Matthew 17:8*

    Hail Mary.

10. As they came down from the mountain Jesus gave them this order, 'Tell no one about the vision until the Son of Man has risen from the dead'. *Matthew 17:9*

    Hail Mary.

**Glory be to the Father.**

# – Christ's Institution of the Eucharist as the Sacramental Expression of the Paschal Mystery –

Our Father.

1. It was before the festival of the Passover, and Jesus knew that the hour had come for him to pass from this world to the Father. He had always loved those who were his in the world, but now he showed how perfect his love was. *John 13:1*

   Hail Mary.

2. Now on the first day of Unleavened Bread the disciples came to Jesus to say, 'Where do you want us to make the preparations for you to eat the passover'? *Matthew 26:17*

   The disciples did what Jesus told them and prepared the Passover. *Matthew 26:19*

   Hail Mary.

3. When the hour came he took his place at table, and the apostles with him. And he said to them, 'I have longed to eat this passover with you before I suffer; because, I tell you, I shall not eat it again until it is fulfilled in the kingdom of God'.

   Hail Mary. *Luke 22:14-16*

4. Then, taking a cup, he gave thanks and said, 'Take this and share it among you, because from now on, I tell you, I shall not drink wine until the kingdom of God comes'. *Luke 22:17-18*

    Hail Mary.

5. Then he took some bread, and when he had given thanks, broke it and gave it to them, saying, 'This is my body which will be given for you; do this as a memorial of me'. *Luke 22:19*

    Hail Mary.

6. He did the same with the cup after supper, and said, 'This cup is the new covenant in my blood which will be poured out for you. *Luke 22:20*

    Hail Mary.

7. 'My little children, I shall not be with you much longer. You will look for me, and, as I told the Jews, where I am going, you cannot come. I give you a new commandment: love one another; just as I have loved you, you also must love one another. By this love you have for one another, everyone will know that you are my disciples.'

    *John 13:33-35*

    Hail Mary.

8. 'Do not let your hearts be troubled. Trust in God still, and trust in me. *John 14:1*

    Hail Mary.

9. There are many rooms in my Father's house; if there were not, I should have told you. I am going now to prepare a place for you, and after I have gone and prepared you a place, I shall return to take you with me; so that where I am you may be too. *John 14:2-3*

   Hail Mary.


10. Father, Righteous One, the world has not known you, but I have known you, and these have known that you have sent me. I have made your name known to them and will continue to make it known, so that the love with which you loved me may be in them, and so that I may be in them.' *John 17:25-26*

    Hail Mary.

**Glory be to the Father.**

# The Sorrowful Mysteries

## – The Agony in the Garden –

Our Father

1. Then Jesus came with them to a small estate called Gethsemane; and he said to his disciples: 'Stay here while I go over there to pray.'
   *Matthew 26:36*

    Hail Mary.

2. He took Peter and the two sons of Zebedee with him. And sadness came over him, and great distress.
   *Matthew 26:37*

    Hail Mary.

3. Then he said to them: 'My soul is sorrowful to the point of death. Wait here and keep awake with me.'
   *Matthew 26:38*

    Hail Mary.

4. And going on a little further he fell on his face and prayed. 'My Father,' he said, 'if it is possible,

let this cup pass me by. Nevertheless, let it be as you, not I, would have it.' *Matthew 26:39*

Hail Mary.

5. He came back to the disciples and found them sleeping, and he said to Peter: 'So you had not the strength to keep awake with me one hour? You should be awake, and praying not to be put to the test. The spirit is willing, but the flesh is weak.' *Matthew 26:40-41*

   Hail Mary.

6. Again a second time, he went away and prayed: 'My Father,' he said, 'if this cup cannot pass by without my drinking it, your will be done!'
   *Matthew 26:42*

   Hail Mary.

7. Then an angel appeared to him, coming from heaven to give him strength. *Luke 22:43*

   Hail Mary.

8. In his anguish he prayed even more earnestly, and his sweat fell to the ground like great drops of blood. *Luke 22:44*

   Hail Mary.

9. When he rose from prayer he went to the disciples and found them sleeping for sheer grief.
   *Luke 22:45*

   'You can sleep on now and take your rest. Now the hour has come when the Son of Man is to be betrayed into the hands of sinners.
   *Matthew 26:45*

   Hail Mary.

10. 'Get up! Let us go! My betrayer is already close at hand.' He was still speaking when Judas, one of the Twelve, appeared, and with him a large number of men armed with swords and clubs, sent by the chief priests and elders of the people.
    *Matthew 26:46-47*

    Hail Mary.

**Glory be to the Father.**

# *– The Scourging of Jesus at the Pillar –*

Our Father

1. So Pilate, anxious to placate the crowd, released Barabbas for them and, having ordered Jesus to be scourged, handed him over to be crucified.
   *Mark 15:15*

   Hail Mary.

2. Now all this happened to fulfil the prophecies in scripture. Then all the disciples deserted him and ran away. *Matthew 26:56*

   Hail Mary.

3. Meanwhile the men who guarded Jesus were mocking and beating him. *Luke 22:63*

   Hail Mary.

4. And yet ours were the sufferings he bore,
   ours the sorrows he carried.
   But we, we thought of him as someone punished,
   struck by God, and brought low.
   Yet he was pierced through for our faults,
   crushed for our sins. *Isaiah 53:4-5*

   Hail Mary.

5. For my part, I made no resistance,
   neither did I turn away.
   I offered my back to those who struck me,
   my cheeks to those who tore at my beard;
   I did not cover my face
   against insult and spittle. *Isaiah 50:5-6*

   Hail Mary.

6. …from the sole of the foot to the head
   there is not a sound spot:
   wounds, bruises, open sores
   not dressed, not bandaged,
   not soothed with oil. *Isaiah 1:6*

   Hail Mary.

7. Ploughmen have ploughed on my back longer
   and longer furrows… *Psalm 129:3*

   Hail Mary.

8. I have trodden the winepress alone.
   Of the men of my people not one was with me.
   *Isaiah 63:3*

   Hail Mary.

9. I will punish their sins with the rod
   and their crimes with the whip… *Psalm 89:32*

   Hail Mary.

10. On him lies a punishment that brings us peace, and through his wounds we are healed.

*Isaiah 53:5*

    Hail Mary.

Glory be to the Father.

## – *The Crowning of Jesus with Thorns* –

Our Father.

1. The soldiers led him away to the inner part of the palace, that is, the Praetorium, and called the whole cohort together. *Mark 15:16*

    Hail Mary.

2. …and after this, the soldiers twisted some thorns into a crown and put it on his head, and dressed him in a purple robe. *John 19:2*

    Hail Mary.

3. They kept coming up to him and saying: 'Hail, king of the Jews!' and they slapped him in the face. *John 19:3*

    Hail Mary.

4. If the virtuous man is God's son, God will take his part
and rescue him from the clutches of his enemies.
Let us test him with cruelty and with torture,
and thus explore this gentleness of his
and put his endurance to the proof.

*Wisdom 2:18-19*

    Hail Mary.

5. They struck his head with a reed and spat on him; and they went down on their knees to do him homage.

*Mark 15:19*

    Hail Mary.

6. Jesus then came out wearing the crown of thorns and the purple robe. Pilate said: 'Here is the man.'

*John 19:5*

    Hail Mary.

7. As the crowds were appalled on seeing him
so disfigured did he look
that he seemed no longer human –
so will the crowds be astonished at him,
and kings stand speechless before him;
for they shall see something never told
and witness something never heard before:

*Isaiah 52:14-15*

    Hail Mary.

8. And when they had finished making fun of him, they took off the cloak and dressed him in his own clothes. *Matthew 27:31*

    Hail Mary.

9. Let us condemn him to a shameful death since he will be looked after – we have his word for it. *Wisdom 2:20*

    Hail Mary.

10. So in the end Pilate handed him over to them to be crucified. *John 19:16*

    Hail Mary.

**Glory be to the Father.**

# – *Jesus Carries His Cross* –

Our Father.

1. They led him out to crucify him. *Mark 15:21*

    Hail Mary.

2. As they were leading him away they seized on a man, Simon from Cyrene, who was coming in from the country, and made him shoulder the cross and carry it behind Jesus. *Luke 23:26*

    Hail Mary.

3. Large numbers of people followed him, and of women too, who mourned and lamented for him.
*Luke 23:27*

    Hail Mary.

4. But Jesus turned to them and said: 'Daughters of Jerusalem, do not weep for me;
*Luke 23:28*

    Hail Mary.

5. '…weep rather for yourselves and for your children. *Luke 23:28*

    Hail Mary.

6. 'For the days will surely come when people will say: "Happy are those who are barren, the wombs that have never borne, the breasts that have

never suckled!" Then they will begin to say to the mountains: "Fall on us!", to the hills, "Cover us!" For if men use the green wood like this, what will happen when it is dry?' *Luke 23:29-31*

    Hail Mary.

7. We had all gone astray like sheep,
   each taking his own way,.
   and Yahweh burdened him
   with the sins of all of us. *Isaiah 53:7*

       Hail Mary.

8. Harshly dealt with, he bore it humbly,
   he never opened his mouth,
   like a lamb that is led to the slaughter-house,
   like a sheep that is dumb before its shearers
   never opening its mouth. *Isaiah 53:6*

       Hail Mary.

9. Now with him they were also leading out two other criminals to be executed. *Luke 23:32*

       Hail Mary.

10. They brought Jesus to the place called Golgotha, which means the place of the skull. *Mark 15:22*

Hail Mary.

**Glory be to the Father.**

# – *The Crucifixion* –

Our Father.

1. When they had reached a place called Golgotha, that is, the place of the skull, they gave him wine to drink mixed with gall, which he tasted but refused to drink. *Matthew 27:33-34*

    Hail Mary.

2. It was the third hour when they crucified him.
*Mark 15:25*

    When they had finished crucifying him they shared out his clothing by casting lots, and then sat down and stayed there keeping guard over him. *Matthew 27:35-36*

    Hail Mary.

3. Above his head was placed the charge against him; it read: 'This is Jesus, the King of the Jews.' At the same time two robbers were crucified with him, one on the right and one on the left.

    *Matthew 27:37-38*

    Hail Mary.

4. The passers-by jeered at him: *Matthew 27:39*

    One of the criminals hanging there abused him. 'Are you not the Christ?' he said. 'Save yourself and us as well.' But the other spoke up and rebuked him. 'Have you no fear of God at all?' he said. 'You got the same sentence as he did, but in

our case we deserved it: we are paying for what we did. But this man has done nothing wrong. Jesus', he said, 'remember me when you come into your Kingdom.' 'Indeed, I promise you,' he replied, 'today you will be with me in paradise.'
*Luke 23:39-43*

    Hail Mary.

5. Near the cross of Jesus stood his mother and his mother's sister, Mary the wife of Clopas, and Mary of Magdala. Seeing his mother and the disciple he loved standing near her, Jesus said to his mother: 'Woman, this is your son.' Then to the disciple he said: 'This is your mother'. And from that moment the disciple made a place for her in his home. *John 19:25-27*

    Hail Mary.

6. It was now about the sixth hour and, with the sun eclipsed, a darkness came over the whole land until the ninth hour. The veil of the Temple was torn right down the middle. *Luke 23:44-45*

    Hail Mary.

7. And about the ninth hour, Jesus cried out in a loud voice: 'Eli, Eli, lama sabachthani?' that is: 'My God, my God, why have you deserted me?'
*Matthew 27:46*

    Hail Mary.

8. After this, Jesus knew that everything had now been completed, and to fulfil the scripture perfectly he said: 'I am thirsty.'
   A jar full of vinegar stood there, so putting a sponge soaked in the vinegar on a hyssop stick they held it up to his mouth. *John 19:28-29*

   Hail Mary.

9. After Jesus had taken the vinegar he said: 'It is accomplished;' and bowing his head he gave up his spirit. *John 19:30*

   Hail Mary.

10. When the centurion saw what had taken place, he gave praise to God and said: 'This was a great and good man.' And when all the people who had gathered for the spectacle saw what had happened, they went home beating their breasts.
    *Luke 23:47-48*

    Hail Mary.

**Glory be to the Father.**

# The Glorious Mysteries

## – The Resurrection –

Our Father.

1. When the Sabbath was over, Mary of Magdala, Mary the mother of James, and Salome, bought spices with which to go and anoint him. And very early in the morning on the first day of the week they went to the tomb, just as the sun was rising. *Mark 16:1-2*

    Hail Mary.

2. And all at once there was a violent earthquake, for the angel of the Lord, descending from heaven, came and rolled away the stone and sat on it. His face was like lightning, his robe white as snow. The guards were so shaken, so frightened of him, that they were like dead men.
*Matthew 28:2-4*

    Hail Mary.

3. But the angel spoke; and he said to the women: 'There is no need for you to be afraid. I know you

are looking for Jesus, who was crucified. He is not here, for he has risen, as he said he would. Come and see the place where he lay, then go quickly and tell his disciples: "He has risen from the dead and now he is going before you to Galilee; it is there you will see him." Now I have told you.' *Matthew 28:5-7*

Hail Mary.

4. Filled with awe and great joy the women came quickly away from the tomb and ran to tell the disciples. And there, coming to meet them, was Jesus. 'Greetings,' he said. And the women came up to him and, falling down before him, clasped his feet. *Matthew 28:8-9*

    Hail Mary.

5. Then Jesus said to them: 'Do not be afraid; go and tell my brothers that they must leave for Galilee; they will see me there.' *Matthew 28:10*

    Hail Mary.

6. In the evening of that same day, the first day of the week, the doors were closed in the room where the disciples were, for fear of the Jews. Jesus came and stood among them. He said to them: 'Peace be with you.' *John 20:19*

    Hail Mary.

7. In a state of alarm and fright, they thought they were seeing a ghost. But he said: 'Why are you so agitated, and why are these doubts rising in your hearts? Look at my hands and feet; yes, it is I indeed. Touch me and see for yourselves; a ghost has no flesh and bones as you can see I have.'
*Luke 24:37-39*

   Hail Mary.

8. And as he said this he showed them his hands and feet. Their joy was so great that they still could not believe it, and they stood there dumbfounded; so he said to them: 'Have you anything here to eat?' And they offered him a piece of grilled fish, which he took and ate before their eyes. *Luke 24:40-43*

   Hail Mary.

9. Then he told them: 'This is what I meant when I said, while I was still with you, that everything written about me in the Law of Moses, in the Prophets and in the Psalms, has to be fulfilled.' He then opened their minds to understand the scriptures… *Luke 24:44-45*

   Hail Mary.

10. …and he said to them: 'So you see how it is written that the Christ would suffer and on the third day rise from the dead, and that, in his

name, repentance for the forgiveness of sins would be preached to all the nations, beginning from Jerusalem. You are witnesses to this.'

*Luke 24:46-48*

    Hail Mary.

**Glory be to the Father.**

## – *The Ascension* –

Our Father.

1. He had shown himself alive to them after his Passion by many demonstrations: for forty days he had continued to appear to them and tell them about the kingdom of God. *Acts 1:3*

    Hail Mary.

2. …the eleven disciples set out for Galilee, to the mountain where Jesus had arranged to meet them. When they saw him they fell down before him, though some hesitated. *Matthew 28:16-17*

    Hail Mary.

3. Jesus came up and spoke to them. He said: 'All authority in heaven and on earth has been given to me...'   *Matthew 28:18*

   Hail Mary.

4. 'Go, therefore, make disciples of all the nations; baptize them in the name of the Father and of the Son and of the Holy Spirit...'   *Matthew 28:19*

   Hail Mary.

5. '...and teach them to observe all the commands I gave you. And know that I am with you always; yes, to the end of time.'   *Matthew 28:20*

   Hail Mary.

6. As he said this he was lifted up while they looked on, and a cloud took him from their sight.   *Acts 1:9*

   Hail Mary.

7. And so the Lord Jesus, after he had spoken to them, was taken up into heaven: there at the right hand of God he took his place,   *Mark 16:19*

   Hail Mary.

8. They were still staring into the sky when suddenly two men in white were standing near them.   *Acts 1:10*

   Hail Mary.

9. ...and they said: 'Why are you men from Galilee standing here looking into the sky? Jesus who has been taken up from you into heaven, this same Jesus will come back in the same way as you have seen him go there.' *Acts 1:11*

   Hail Mary.

10. So from the Mount of Olives, as it is called, they went back to Jerusalem, a short distance away, no more than a Sabbath walk; *Acts 1:12*

    Hail Mary.

**Glory be to the Father.**

# *– The Descent of the Holy Spirit –*

Our Father.

1. 'And now I am sending down to you what the Father has promised. Stay in the city then, until you are clothed with power from on high.'

   *Luke 24:49*

   Hail Mary.

2. ...and when they reached the city they went to the upper room where they were staying; ...All these (the eleven apostles) joined in continuous prayer, together with several women, including Mary the mother of Jesus, and with his brothers.

   *Acts 1:13-14*

   Hail Mary.

3. When Pentecost day came round, they had all met in one room, when suddenly they heard what sounded like a powerful wind from heaven, the noise of which filled the entire house in which they were sitting; and something appeared to them that seemed like tongues of fire; these separated and came to rest on the head of each of them.

   *Acts 2:1-3*

   Hail Mary.

4. They were all filled with the Holy Spirit, and began to speak foreign languages as the Spirit

gave them the gift of speech. Now there were devout men living in Jerusalem from every nation under heaven, and at this sound they all assembled, each one bewildered to hear these men speaking his own language. *Acts 2:4-6*

    Hail Mary.

5. Everyone was amazed and unable to explain it; they asked one another what it all meant. Some, however, laughed it off. 'They have been drinking too much new wine,' they said. *Acts 2:12-13*

    Hail Mary.

6. Then Peter stood up with the Eleven and addressed them in a loud voice:
'…this is what the prophet spoke of:
In the days to come – it is the Lord who speaks –
I will pour out my spirit on all mankind.
Their sons and daughters shall prophesy,
your young men shall see visions,
your old men shall dream dreams.
Even on my slaves, men and women,
in those days, I will pour out my spirit…'
*Acts 2:14, 16-18*

    Hail Mary.

7. 'God raised this man Jesus to life, and all of us are witnesses to that. Now raised to the heights by God's right hand, he has received from the Father

the Holy Spirit, who was promised, and what you see and hear is the outpouring of that Spirit.'

Hail Mary. *Acts 2:32-33*

8. '…the whole House of Israel can be certain that God has made this Jesus whom you crucified both Lord and Christ.' Hearing this, they were cut to the heart and said to Peter and the apostles: 'What must we do, brothers?' 'You must repent,' Peter answered, 'and every one of you must be baptised in the name of Jesus Christ for the forgiveness of your sins, and you will receive the gift of the Holy Spirit.' *Acts 2:36-38*

Hail Mary.

9. 'The promise that was made is for you and your children, and for all those who are far away, for all those whom the Lord our God will call to himself.'

Hail Mary. *Acts 2:39*

10. He spoke to them for a long time using many arguments, and he urged them: 'Save yourselves from this perverse generation.' They were convinced by his arguments, and they accepted what he said and were baptised. That very day about three thousand were added to their number.

Hail Mary. *Acts 2:40-41*

**Glory be to the Father.**

# – *The Assumption of Our Lady* –

Our Father.

1. But Christ has in fact been raised from the dead, the first-fruits of all who have fallen asleep… Just as all men die in Adam, so all men will be brought to life in Christ; but all of them in their proper order: Christ as the first-fruits and then, after the coming of Christ, those who belong to him. *1 Corinthians 15:20, 22-23*

    Hail Mary.

2. When this perishable nature has put on imperishability, and when this mortal nature has put on immortality, then the words of the scripture will come true: Death is swallowed up in victory. Death, where is your victory? Death, where is your sting? Now the sting of death is sin, and sin gets its power from the Law. So let us thank God for giving us the victory through our Lord Jesus Christ. *1 Corinthians 15:54-57*

    Hail Mary.

3. …the ones he chose specially long ago and intended to become true images of his Son, so that his Son might be the eldest of many brothers.

He called those he intended for this; those he called justified, and with those he justified he shared his glory. *Romans 8:29-30*

    Hail Mary.

4. For we know that when the tent that we live in on earth is folded up, there is a house built by God for us, an everlasting home not made by human hands, in the heavens. *2 Corinthians 5:1*

       Hail Mary.

5. Now a great sign appeared in heaven: a woman, adorned with the sun, standing on the moon, and with the twelve stars on her head for a crown. *Revelation 12:1*

       Hail Mary.

6. May you be blessed, my daughter,
   by God Most High,
   beyond all women on earth;
   and may the Lord God be blessed,
   the Creator of heaven and earth,
   by whose guidance you cut off the head
   of the leader of our enemies. *Judith 13:23-24*

       Hail Mary.

7. The trust you have shown
   shall not pass from the memories of men,

but shall ever remind them of the power of God.
God grant you to be always held in honour,
and rewarded with blessings, *Judith 13:25*

    Hail Mary.

8. You are the glory of Jerusalem!
You are the great pride of Israel!
You are the highest honour of our race!
May you be blessed by the Lord Almighty
in all the days to come! *Judith 15:10*

    Hail Mary.

9. Who is this arising like the dawn,
fair as the moon,
resplendent as the sun,
terrible as an army with banners?
Who is this coming up from the desert
leaning on her Beloved? *Song of Songs 6:9, 8:5*

    Hail Mary.

10. For Yahweh has chosen Zion,
desiring this to be his home:
Here I will stay for ever,
this is the home I have chosen. *Psalm 132:13-14*

    Hail Mary.

**Glory be to the Father.**

# – *The Crowning of Our Lady in Heaven* –

Our Father.

1. Your throne, God, shall last for ever and ever,
   you royal sceptre is a sceptre of integrity:
   virtue you love as much as you hate wickedness.

   *Psalm 45:6-7*

   Hail Mary.

2. This is why God, your God, has anointed you
   with the oil of gladness, above all your rivals;
   myrrh and aloes waft from your robes. *Psalm 45:7-8*

   Hail Mary.

3. From palaces of ivory harps entertain you,
   daughters of kings are among your maids of
   honour, on your right stands the queen, in gold
   from Ophir.              *Psalm 45:8-9*

   Hail Mary.

4. I came forth from the mouth of the Most High,
   and I covered the earth like a mist.
   I had my tents in the heights,
   and my throne in a pillar of cloud.

   *Ecclesiasticus 24:5-7*

   Hail Mary.

5. Alone I encircled the vault of the sky,
   and I walked on the bottom of the deeps.
   Over the waves of the sea and over the whole earth,
   and over every people and nation I have held sway.

   *Ecclesiasticus 24:8-9*

   Hail Mary.

6. From eternity, in the beginning, he created me,
   and for eternity I shall remain.
   I ministered before him in the holy tabernacle,
   and thus was I established on Zion.
   In the beloved city he has given me rest,
   and in Jerusalem I wield my authority.

   *Ecclesiasticus 24:14-15*

   Hail Mary.

7. Approach me, you who desire me,
   and take your fill of my fruits,
   for memories of me are sweeter than honey,
   inheriting me is sweeter than the honeycomb.

   *Ecclesiasticus 24:26-27*

   Hail Mary.

8. They who eat me will hunger for more,
   they who drink me will thirst for more.
   Whoever listens to me will never have to blush,
   whoever acts as I dictate will never sin.

   *Ecclesiasticus 24:28-30*

   Hail Mary.

9. The King has brought me into his rooms;
   you will be our joy and our gladness.
   We shall praise your love above wine;
   how right it is to love you.

   *Song of Songs 1:4*

   Hail Mary.

10. Let us be confident, then, in approaching the throne of
    grace, that we shall have mercy from him
    and find grace when we are in need of help.

    *Hebrews 4:16*

    Hail Mary.

**Glory be to the Father.**

# Prayer

O God,
    your only begotten Son gained eternal life for us
        by his life, death and resurrection.
    May we who meditate on these mysteries in the
        holy rosary of the blessed Virgin Mary
        both follow the example that they give
        and obtain the salvation that they promise:
            through our Lord Jesus Christ your Son,
            who live and reigns with you
            in the unity of the Holy Spirit,
            one God, for ever and ever. Amen.